For Tom and Jack
H.E.

For Mum and Dad
A.C.

Fun-to-read Picture Books have been
grouped into three approximate readability
levels by Bernice Moon, teacher-in-charge,
Ellington Language and Literacy Centre,
Maidenhead, Berkshire. Yellow books
are suitable for beginners; red books
for readers acquiring first fluency; blue
books for more advanced readers.

This book has been assessed as Stage 5
according to *Individualised Reading,* by
Cliff Moon and Norman Ruel, published by
the Reading and Language Information Centre,
University of Reading.

First published 1988 by
Walker Books Ltd
Walker House
87 Vauxhall Walk
London SE11 5HJ

Text © 1988 Heather Eyles
Illustrations © 1988 Andy Cooke

First printed 1988
Printed in France by
Brodard Graphique

British Library Cataloguing in Publication Data
Eyles, Heather
A Zoo in our house. – (Fun-to-read
picture books series)
I. Title II. Cooke, Andy III. Series
823'.914[J]   PZ7

ISBN 0-7445-0542-9

A ZOO IN OUR HOUSE

WRITTEN BY

Heather Eyles

ILLUSTRATED BY

Andy Cooke

WALKER BOOKS

LONDON

Mom and I went
to the zoo.

I said, "Can we have a zoo in our house?" "Certainly not," said Mom.

But . . .

...on Monday a giraffe
was eating in the kitchen.

On Tuesday a hippopotamus
was splashing in the bath.

On Wednesday a monkey
was swinging in the hall.

On Thursday a crocodile
was washing in the garden.

On Friday a lion
was sleeping in the living room.

On Saturday
all the animals came
and we had a party.

On Sunday Mum sent them
all back to the zoo.

"Phew," said Mom.
But...

...she forgot the gorilla.